Au
Slang

SARAH DAWSON

PENGUIN BOOKS

PENGUIN BOOKS

Published by the Penguin Group
Penguin Group (Australia)
250 Camberwell Road, Camberwell, Victoria 3124, Australia
(a division of Pearson Australia Group Pty Ltd)

Penguin Books Ltd, Registered Offices: 80 Strand, London WC2R 0RL, England

First published by Penguin Books Australia Ltd 1999

24 23 22 21 20 19 18 17 16

Copyright © Penguin Books Australia Ltd 1999

All rights reserved. Without limiting the rights under copyright reserved above, no part
of this publication may be reproduced, stored in or introduced into a retrieval system, or
transmitted, in any form or by any means (electronic, mechanical, photocopying,
recording or otherwise), without the prior written permission of both the copyright
owner and the above publisher of this book.

Cover and text design by Lynn Twelftree
Cover photograph by D & M Trounson/A.N.T. Photo Library
Typeset in Rotis by Midland Typesetters, Maryborough, Victoria
Printed and bound in Australia by McPherson's Printing Group, Maryborough, Victoria

National Library of Australia
Cataloguing-in-Publication data:

Dawson, Sarah.
 Aussie slang.
 ISBN 978 0 14 028689 2.
 1. English language – Australia – Slang. 2. English
 language – Australia – Slang – Humour. I. Title.
427.994

penguin.com.au

Slang is a language that rolls up its sleeves, spits on its hands and goes to work.

Carl Sandburg (1878–1967), poet and folklorist

Introduction

AUSSIE SLANG translates and celebrates Australia's rich and very vivid 'slanguage'. It is intended for locals as well as visitors, because Australia's younger generation and any oldies who have not ventured much 'O.S.' often have no idea quite how alien and incomprehensible their native language is, even to other English-speakers.

Australians do speak English, of course. But to many tourists (and even some locals), Aussie

English has only tenuous links with the mother tongue. Put an English-speaking visitor in a roomful of Aussies or next to a radio without the benefit of an interpreter, and they are likely to be almost at a complete loss to understand what is being said. Of course, this is in part due to the distinctive Australian accent, which makes things hard for non-residents. But even more bewilderingly, everyday Aussie speech is peppered with words and phrases whose arcane meanings are understood only by the initiated. It is these colourful colloquialisms that **AUSSIE SLANG** sets out to explain.

This book doesn't pretend to be a comprehensive dictionary of Australian slang. That would require a very much bigger volume and anyway there are already several more or less academic collections around. But it does offer a vivid selection of the Aussie vernacular at its most inventive and picturesque.

For space reasons, I've favoured dinkum Aussie slang over words or phrases borrowed from other nations. And I have mostly left out expressions which seem to have originated in Oz but were adopted out elsewhere. I've also omitted some colourful sayings which are (fairly) self-explanatory: 'as bald as a bandicoot', 'as dry as a pommy's bath-towel', 'flat out like a lizard drinking', and so on.

Since colonial times, Australia's path of growth, rebellion and self-discovery has been pretty much like that of most offspring. Aussies coined and adopted slang with great gusto, no doubt as a means of cocking a snook at authority and at social niceties favoured by the mother country. As a US War Department guide to Australia for Yank servicemen on 'R and R' leave succinctly put it in 1943, '[Australians] haven't much respect for stuffed-shirts, their own or anyone else's'. Most commentators agree that Australia is unusual in having taken up slang at all levels of society, not just the lower orders.

Aussie slang has a few marked features. Though most Australians live along the coastal fringe and always have, a remarkable number of references to the remote inland have found their way into the vernacular and thence into the national consciousness. Quite a few references to sterling currency (quid, shilling, two bob, zac) have persisted, although this system was replaced by decimal currency as long ago as 1966. A large proportion of Australian slang centres on a small number of topics, notably booze, body parts (especially private ones), bodily evacuations, and sex. There is also more than a sprinkling of sexism and racism, which may mirror the fact that white Australia's cultural origins are chiefly working-class English, a milieu in which females and foreigners are not held in high regard. At the same time, the seemingly endless number of personal insults are more often than not jocular, affectionate even, rather than truly aggressive.

All in all, Aussie slang really isn't meant to be taken too seriously. So relax and enjoy this little collection: it's a bottler.

acre
The buttocks or backside: 'sitting on his acre'.

Adrians *or* **Adrian Quist**
Very drunk. (Rhyming slang for 'pissed'.)
Australians have enthusiastically upheld the English tradition of rhyming slang. Some idiosyncratic Aussie coinages, such as *Joe Blake* (snake) and *Nellie Blighs* (flies) are included in

the body of this book. Other distinctive local usages include *Aristotle* (bottle); *bag of fruit* (suit); *goanna* (piano); *Hawkesbury Rivers* (shivers); *Kerry Packered* (knackered: exhausted, broken); *on the Errol Flynn* (on the chin); *optic nerve* (perve); *rubbity* (rub-a-dub-dub: pub); and *Wally Grout* (shout: to pay for someone else's drinks, etc.). Often an expression is shortened, so that 'Hawkesbury Rivers' may be heard as *Hawkesburies*, or 'Kerry Packered' as *Kerried*, and so on.

aerial pingpong
The name given to Australian Rules football by supporters of the nation's imported football codes, rugby and soccer. Aussie Rules is distinguished by its players' high-flying pursuit of the ball.

Rugby is in turn referred to, by Australian Rules fans, as **cross-country wrestling**.

around the traps
Here and there; out and about: 'We're not exactly mates any more, but I sometimes see him around the traps'.

arse

1 (also *arsehole*) An offensive or objectionable person or thing: 'Don't be such an arse'.
2 The backside or buttocks.

arse, give someone *or* something the
To dismiss or get rid of: 'I've given all your old clothes the arse'.

arvo
Afternoon.

back of Bourke
also *back of beyond*
A very distant or remote place. (Bourke is an
outback town in the far north-west of New
South Wales.)

banana bender
A person from the tropical north-eastern state
of Queensland. The epithet is playful rather
than geographically precise, as the bulk of

Australia's banana crop is in fact grown in neighbouring New South Wales.

bandicoot on a burnt ridge, like a
Miserable or lonely.

bang
As a noun, sexual intercourse. As a verb, to have sexual intercourse.

This word has been incorporated into a range of picturesque expressions, such as *bang like a dunny door in a gale* and *bang like a rattlesnake*, both of which mean to take part in sex very frequently, willingly or vigorously.

barbie

A barbecue. An example of the Australian fondness for shortening words and adding the suffix *-ie* (sometimes *-y*).

Some particular favourites, such as *blowie*, *brekkie*, *cozzie*, *pollie*, *sickie* and *sunnies*, are noted in their rightful place in the course of this book. Other examples include *gladdie* (the gladiolus, well publicised by satirist Barry Humphries' alter ego Edna Everage); *lippy* (lipstick); *rellies* (relatives); *postie* (person who delivers mail); *prezzie* (a present); and *trammie* (a tram driver, traditionally assisted by a *connie* or conductor).

For comments on the similar use of the suffix *-o*, see **garbo**.

barrack

As a spectator, to support or encourage one's team, usually noisily. This is almost the exact opposite of the original English meaning, to sneer at or insult players, presumably (but not necessarily) those on the opposing team.

battler

often used in the phrase *little Aussie battler*
The average hard-working Aussie, especially one struggling to make ends meet. This is an image used more by Australian politicians than by the battlers themselves. (In colonial times *a battler* was the term for an inefficient or unsuccessful farmer.)

beaut!, beauty! *or* **bewdy!**
A cry of delight or total approval. It is often paired with 'mate' or 'bottler' (the latter itself an expression of approval), as in 'Bewdy, bottler!'.

bible-basher
A person who is fervently or fanatically religious.

big bikkies
A lot of money: 'That car's worth big bikkies'. (*Bikkie/bickie* is a diminutive of 'biscuit'.)

big on
Very fond of or enthusiastic about: 'They're big on junk food'.

bike, the town
also *the local bike*
A female generous with her sexual favours.

bikie
A motorbike rider, especially one who is a member of a group or gang.

bingle
A vehicle accident, usually a minor rather than a major one.

bitser

A mixed-breed dog or, by extension, a person of mixed parentage.

bizzo

Business: 'Mind your own bizzo, mate!'.

black stump

An imaginary, very remote place in the outback.

block

The head, or more particularly what lies in it. This may be one's brain or intelligence: 'Use your block!'. Or it may refer to one's good humour or temper: 'She lost [or 'did'] her block and chucked in her job'.

blow through
To go or disappear, especially without notice.

blowhard
A talkative or boastful person.

blowie
A blowfly.

bludge
To loaf or be lazy when one should be working.
More often than not, the term *bludger* refers to
someone taking advantage of the welfare
system.

blue

1 A fight or argument: 'I could hear them having a blue'.
2 A mistake or blunder: 'That was a real blue'.

bluey

1 A police summons to appear in court, or a duplicate copy of the charges against the defendant. (The paper is blue.)
2 (also *Blue*) Term of address for a person with red hair: 'G'day, Bluey!'.

bogan

A stupid or uncouth person.

Bondi tram

Trams no longer run in the Sydney suburb of Bondi, so (as with **Mallee bull**) this is a figurative expression only.

If you *shoot through like a Bondi tram*, you depart rapidly and usually without warning. (Trams on the Bondi route were notoriously speedy.) If you have *a face like a Bondi tram*, you are not rated very attractive.

bonzer/bonza

An adjective expressing great enthusiasm or approval: 'a bonzer bloke'. It is not widely used nowadays, other than in books or films depicting the stereotypic Aussie.

boozer

1 A person who drinks excessive quantities of alcohol.

2 A pub.

boss cocky

The boss or person in charge.

bot

To borrow or beg, usually without planning to repay. *A bot* is someone who does this rather too often.

bottler

An expression of delight or absolute approval. A synonym for **beauty**!

bottom-of-the-harbour scheme
An illicit financial stratagem designed to evade tax, usually involving the sale of a company in such a way that its accounts cannot be traced.

brasco
A lavatory.

breezer
A fart.

brekkie/brekky
Breakfast.

bronze
The anus or backside: 'sitting on your bronze'.

Buckley's chance

No chance at all. (Variously thought to derive from the former Melbourne department store Buckley & Nunn; or from William Buckley, a convict of the early nineteenth century who escaped from captivity but was later recaptured. The latter explanation seems more likely.)

bull *or* bullshit

also *bulldust* and occasionally *bull's-wool*
Nonsense, or meaningless or exaggerated talk: 'He is full of bullshit'.

Bullshit can also be a verb ('Stop bullshitting'), or be expanded to *bullshitter* to describe a person who habitually does so.

bundy
Bundaberg rum. (Bundaberg is the name of the brand and of the Queensland city in which it is made.)

bung
To put: 'She can really bung on the charm when she needs to'.

bung, go
To break down, collapse or stop functioning properly: 'My car went bung yesterday'.

bush telegraph
also *bush wireless* or *mulga wire*
The grapevine; a network for passing on rumours or gossip.

bush week
Most commonly heard in the scoffing rejoinder
'What d'you think it is, bush week?', which
means that the speaker isn't easily fooled
or deceived. It is usually a response to a
questionable statement or unreasonable
request.

bushed
1 Lost or bewildered.
2 Very tired.

bushfire blonde
A person with red hair.

bushie

also *bushwhacker*

A person from the countryside or sparsely populated inland. By extension it may also mean anyone who is unsophisticated or uncultured.

butchers

short for *butcher's hook*

1 A look. (Rhyming slang: this is the original English meaning.)
2 Unwell, or angry. (Rhyming slang for **crook**.)

BYO

Short for 'bring your own [alcohol]', this indicates a restaurant which does not sell alcohol but where diners may bring and consume their own.

The expression has spread to household usage: what you are invited or expected to bring (food, equipment, etc.) is usually evident from the context.

cackleberry
An egg.

carn, the . . . (Saints, Pies, etc.)!
A cry of encouragement from sports spectators,
frequently heard at football matches. (Short for
'Come on, the . . . !'.)

centre, the
also *the red centre*
Central Australia, the arid heart of the
continent. It is generally deemed to include
northern South Australia and most of the
Northern Territory.

chiacking
pronounced **shy**-acking
A round of jeering or sneering.

chockers
Very full. (A variation on 'chock-full'.)

choof off
To leave or go.

chook
A chicken: 'roast chook for dinner'. Also,
by extension and usually less than politely,
a woman.

Someone who *couldn't organise a chook
raffle* is judged to be very incompetent.

chuck or **chunder**
To vomit.

chuck a fit
also *chuck a wobbly*
To become furious or enraged.

city slicker
An urban-dweller.

Claytons
Imitation or specious. (Claytons is a brand of non-alcoholic drink.)

cluey
Clever or well-informed.

cobber
1 A friend or mate.
2 A classic term of address for just about anyone: 'G'day, cobber!'.

cockie/cocky
A small-scale farmer. *A cow cockie* is a dairy farmer.

Collins Street farmer
also (in New South Wales) *a Pitt Street farmer*
An urban resident, usually one in a lucrative profession, who owns a farm chiefly or wholly to lessen his or her income-tax bill. This sense has been extended to suggest any city-dweller who affects the garb and appearance of a country resident.

come good
1 To recover: 'I was crook last week, but I've come good now'.

2 To produce something, especially in response to a request: 'Dad came good with some cash'.

cop shop
A police station.

cot-case
A person who is exhausted or very unwell, though not necessarily bed-ridden.

cow
Something unpleasant or unwanted: 'What a cow of a day!'.

cozzie/cossie
A bathing costume.

crack *or* **crack it**

To succeed at or achieve something: 'Did you crack it to their party?'.

crack a fat

To have an erection.

crap on

To talk incessantly, irritatingly or in a rambling way.

crash-hot

Very good or well: 'I'm not feeling all that crash-hot today'.

crook, be *or* **feel**

To be or feel unwell or below par.

crook, go
To berate or express anger: 'The teacher really
went crook at us'.

cross–country wrestling
also *open-air wrestling*
The derisive name given to rugby by fans of
Australian Rules football. Just as Australian
Rules is known for its airborne leaps, rugby is
characterised by terrestrial scrums and violent
tackles. See also **aerial pingpong**.

crow–eater
A person from South Australia. That state's
Australian Football League team is dubbed 'the
Adelaide Crows'.

crown jewels
also *family jewels*
A man's genitalia.

cubby *or* **cubby-house**
A children's playhouse.

curly one, a
A tricky or difficult question or hypothesis.

Dad and Dave
A shave. (Rhyming slang. Dad and Dave were
the famous fictional characters created by
Australian writer Steele Rudd.)

dag
1 A witty or amusing person: 'You'll like him –
   he's a real dag'.
2 A **daggy** person.

daggy
Unfashionable, drab or downright dull: 'That jacket makes you look really daggy'.

daks
Trousers or pants. Hence *underdaks* are underpants.

dead horse
Sauce, especially tomato sauce, that staple of the Aussie barbie. (Rhyming slang.)

dead marine
An empty beer bottle.

dead ringer
A person or thing that is almost a replica
of another.

death adders in the pocket, have
also *have mouse traps* or *scorpions in the
pocket*
A reason why someone is miserly with their
money: it may be offered as an explanation
or an excuse.

decko/dekko
A look: 'Have a decko at this!'.

demo
A demonstration.

dick, had the
See **had the dick**.

dickless Tracy
A policewoman.

digger
1 Like **cobber**, a friendly term of address.
2 An Australian or New Zealand soldier.

dingbat
An eccentric or mildly crazy person. *The dingbats* are the symptoms displayed by such a person.

dink
also *double-dink*
To carry a passenger on one's bike.

dinkum *or* **dinky-di**
also *fair dinkum*
Genuine, honest, true or truthful.

dip one's lid
To express respect or admiration, originally by
doffing one's hat.

dip out (on)
To do without or to fail to do, get or take part
in: 'I'll dip out on breakfast, thanks'.

do one's dash
To lose out, often as a result of overdoing
things.

dob in *or* **dob on**
To inform or tell tales on: 'You shouldn't dob on
your mates'. *A dobber* does this regularly or
repeatedly.

doco
pronounced **dock**-o
A documentary, especially a film.

Don, the
Sir Donald Bradman, an Australian test cricketer
of the 1920s to 1940s who remained a popular
hero thereafter.

The epithet *the Dons*, on the other hand,
refers to the Australian Football League team
Essendon.

dong
To hit.

don't come the raw prawn!
A derisive response meaning 'Don't try to fool
[or deceive] me'. Not even Australians are
absolutely agreed about the origins of this
expression.

doover
A thingummybob or other thing you can't find a name for.

dosh
Money or cash: 'Can you lend me some dosh?'.

dot
The backside or bottom: 'sitting on one's dot'.

drain the dragon
also *syphon the python*
To urinate.

drink with the flies
To drink alone.

drive the porcelain bus
To vomit into a lavatory, gripping the bowl with
both hands as one does so. There is an implicit
suggestion that the afflicted person has had an
excess of alcohol.

drongo
A foolish or useless person.

droob
A nerd or dull person.

drover's dog
A person of no importance or interest.

dunny
A lavatory.

earbash
To talk endlessly or boringly. *An earbashing*
is thus a long or boring discourse.

eighteen bob in the pound, only
also *a shilling short of a quid*
Crazy, or having lower than normal intelligence.
For further variations on this theme, see **not
the full quid** and **snag short of a barbie**.

emu

A person who chooses or is delegated to pick up discarded items or rubbish in a public place.

enzedder

A New Zealander (from the abbreviation N.Z.).

esky

Often used to mean any portable cooler for food and drinks. (Esky is the brand-name of one such product.)

fair dinkum
See **dinkum**.

fair go! *or* **fair crack of the whip!**
also *fair suck of the sauce bottle!*
or *fair suck of the sav!*
An appeal to someone to be more fair or
reasonable.

FAQ
1 Of average quality. (An acronym: fair average quality.)
2 Frequently asked questions. (Also an acronym, commonly used as shorthand on the Internet.)

five-finger discount
Shoplifting.

flake *or* **flake out**
To pass out, often but not always as the result of being drunk.

flog one's chops
To wear out or exhaust oneself.

flog the log
To masturbate.

footie
Football.

freckle
The anus or backside.

fuckwit
also *fuck-knuckle*
A stupid, ridiculous or otherwise contemptible
person.

full as a boot (or **a goog, tick,** etc.)
Very drunk.

fun of Cork, have the
To enjoy oneself enormously.

furphy
A misleading or unlikely story; a rumour.

G, the

Fond abbreviation of 'MCG' – the Melbourne Cricket Ground, that city's key playing venue for cricket and football. Commentators have dubbed other main ovals in the same way, notably *the Gabba* (in the Brisbane suburb of Woollongabba) and *the Wacka* (HQ of the Western Australian Cricket Association, in Perth).

galah

Any person, but especially a foolish or absurd one.

garbo

A garbage removalist. Another example of the Aussie penchant for abbreviating words, the suffix *-o* being just about as popular as *-ie* (see **barbie**). Some common examples include *compo* (compensation); *kero* (kerosene); *lezzo* (lesbian); *metho* (methylated spirits); *muso* (musician); *politico* (politician); *reffo* (refugee); *rego* (registration) and *Salvos* (the Salvation Army).

g'day
Cheery short form of 'good day', i.e. hello.

geek
1 (also *gig*) A look: 'Take a geek at this!'.
2 A stupid or foolish person: 'Don't be such a geek'.

get on one's tits
To irritate or annoy.

get stuck into
To attack or tackle: 'Let's get stuck into the gardening before it gets too hot'.

give it a bash
also *give it a burl* or *a lash*
To make an attempt, not necessarily with much
confidence in succeeding.

give someone *or* **something the heave**
To reject, get rid of or discard.

give the ferret a run
To have sexual intercourse. ('Ferret' and 'trouser
ferret' are lasting euphemisms for the penis.)

go bush
To go out of circulation or into hiding, or simply
off the main track.

go into smoke
To disappear.

gong, had the
See **had the dick**.

good-oh!
Okay! All right!

goog
An egg. See also **full as a boot**.

Great White Shark
Australian golfer Greg Norman. Probably derived
from his blond hair and the fact that in his
heyday he was deemed to eat up his
competitors.

greenie

An environmentalist or person with 'green' sympathies.

guts

1 As a noun, a greedy person. As a verb, to eat ravenously or excessively.
2 For *rough as guts*, see **rough as bags**.

had the dick
also *had the sword* or *had the gong*
To have broken down or be useless and beyond
remedy: 'My car's really had the dick this time'.

halfback flanker
A wanker; a conceited or arrogant person.
(Rhyming slang.)

hard word, put the ... on
To **put the bite on**.

have someone on
1 To fight.
2 To tease or trick: 'It can't be true. You're
  having me on!'.

have the goods on
To have useful or incriminating information
about.

have tickets on oneself
To be very vain or conceited.

hide

Nerve or cheek: 'You've got a hide to ask for more money!'. Sometimes used in the phrase *more hide than an elephant* (or *than Jessie*: Jessie was an elephant housed at Sydney's Taronga Zoo early in the twentieth century).

hoe into

To tackle or attack energetically.

hoick

To spit.

hooley dooley!

An exclamation of surprise or triumph.

hoon
A ruffian or ill-mannered show-off.

hooroo!
also *oo-roo!*
Goodbye!

hot to trot
Eager to start.

humdinger
A marvellous or excellent person or thing:
'It's a little humdinger!'.

hump
To carry. (From the historical usage 'hump
one's bluey', a bluey being the bundle carried
by a tramp.)

humpy
A hut or shack.

iffy
Questionable, doubtful or risky.

improve, on the
Improving; getting better.

in for one's chop
Ready for or seeking one's share of something.

in like Flynn

Eager or fast to act, especially in relation to sex. (After Errol Flynn, an Australian film star of the 1930s and 1940s whose sexual exploits were well publicised.)

jack of
Irritated with or sick of.

jamberoo
A drinking spree.

jim-jams
Pyjamas: one of many suburban colloquialisms immortalised by satirist Barry Humphries.

Jimmy Brit
Shit. (Rhyming slang.)

Jimmy Woodser
A lone drinker, especially in a bar. (In a country of gregarious pub drinkers, the term implies criticism rather than sympathy.)

Joe Blake, a
A snake. (Rhyming slang.)

Joe Blakes, the
Delirium tremens. (Rhyming slang for 'the shakes'.)

joey
A small or insignificant person or thing, such as a harmless lie. (A joey is a baby kangaroo.)

Johnny Bliss
Piss. (Rhyming slang.)

joker
A person or bloke: 'You're a sociable joker'.

journo
A journalist. For some more examples of the national attachment to the suffix -o, see **garbo**.

kanakas
Testicles.

kangaroos in the top paddock, keep
also *a few kangaroos loose in the* ...
To be dull-witted or of below-average
intelligence.

kick on
To continue partying or having fun.

kid-stakes
Anything small or trivial. The phrase *cut the kid-stakes* is apparently unrelated and means 'Stop that nonsense!'.

king-hit
To hit or punch suddenly and forcefully, usually from behind.

knock
To have sexual intercourse.

knock back
To refuse: 'They knocked back our invitation'. Thus *a knock-back* is a refusal or rejection.

knock off
1 To seduce or have sex with.
2 To stop or finish: 'What time do you knock
   off work?'.

knocker, on the
Promptly: 'We have to be there at seven
on the knocker'.

knockers
Breasts.

knuckle, go the
To fight, especially with the fists.

larrikin
A wild, unruly or undisciplined person.

Larry Dooley, give someone (the)
To chastise, physically or verbally. (Larry Dooley was an Australian boxer.)

lob in
To arrive, especially unannounced or unexpectedly.

lolly, do one's
also *be* or *go off one's lolly*
To become extremely angry.

lolly-water
A soft drink.

look down on the unemployed
(of a man) To urinate.

lose one's meal
To vomit.

lumbered with, get *or* **be**
To be left or burdened with: 'We were
lumbered with cleaning up'.

lurk, a good
sometimes also *not a bad lurk*
A profitable or otherwise rewarding scheme or
situation: 'You only work three days a week?
That's a good lurk!'.

Mallee bull, fit as a
Very fit or in robust health. (Mallee is the name given to arid parts of southern and south-eastern Australia where mallee eucalypts are the main form of vegetation. Presumably the animals there are hardy specimens.)

A person may also *charge like a Mallee bull* (i.e. overcharge), or *be as randy as a Mallee bull* (be oversexed). See also **mallee root**.

mallee root

A prostitute. (Rhyming slang.)

    To *have a face like a mallee root* is to have a gnarled and unbeautiful face. (Mallee is the name given to an unusual form of Australian eucalypt adapted to very dry soil, which has knotted underground stems.)

map of Tasmania

The hair covering the female genital area, deemed to resemble the (roughly triangular) shape of Australia's southernmost island state.

mick

A Roman Catholic.

mix it
To fight.

molies
pronounced **mole**-eez
Short for moleskin trousers, traditionally stockmen's apparel but now worn by many urban-dwellers.

molly-dooker/molly-duker
A left-handed person.

Morts Dock
Cock; penis. (Rhyming slang.)

motsa/motza

also *motser* or *motzer*

A lot of money, especially gambling winnings.

mozzie

A mosquito.

mud map

A rough or sketchy map. (Originally a map drawn on the ground by a stockman.)

muddie

A Queensland mud crab, also known as a mangrove crab and considered a culinary delicacy.

mulga, the

Any remote region. By extension, *mulga madness* is mental derangement owing to extreme isolation. (Mulga is a common name for the scrubby vegetation typical of dry inland areas.)

For *mulga wire*, see **bush telegraph**.

narked *or* **narky**
Irritable or in a bad mood.

ned
1 The head: 'Use your ned!'.
2 See **red ned.**

neddies, the
Horses, especially racehorses or horse-racing
generally: 'a flutter on the neddies'.

nellie
Wine, especially cheap or inferior wine.

Nellie Blighs
Flies, especially blowflies. (Rhyming slang.)

Nellie Melba, do a
A repeated undertaking to leave, never fulfilled.
(Coined for the succession of 'farewell' concerts
reputedly given by Australian singer Nellie
Melba in the 1930s.)

new chum
1 A recently arrived immigrant, especially one
   from the UK.
2 A beginner.

nick, do a
To flee or escape.

no flies on
Said of a person considered shrewd or smart:
'There are no flies on her!'.

no-hoper
A person who is a failure or a loser.

no worries!
Don't worry! An expression of cheerful
reassurance.

Noah *or* **Noah's Ark**
A shark. (Rhyming slang.)

nong *or* **ning-nong**
A silly or stupid person.

norks *or* **norgies**
Breasts.

not much chop
Not very good.

not the full quid
also *not the full bottle*
Not completely sane, or of lower-than-average intelligence.

nuddy, in the
Nude or naked.

ocker
The stereotypic Australian, uncivilised and uncouth. Hence *ockerdom* and *ockerism* denote any or all such characteristics.

off one's brain
also *off one's head* or *off one's scone*
Raving or upset, often with anger.

off one's face
Out of control, especially under the influence of alcohol or drugs.

oil-rag or **oily rag, on the smell of an**
Using very little money, fuel, etc.: 'living on the smell of an oil-rag'.

on a good wicket
In a situation that is, or is likely to be, useful or profitable.

on one's Pat
Alone. (Short for 'on one's Pat Malone': rhyming slang.)

on the Murray
On credit. (Short for *on the Murray cod*: rhyming slang for the colloquialism 'on the nod'.)

on the nose
Smelly. Also, by extension, unpopular or unwanted: 'I'm a bit on the nose with my boss today'.

on ya!
Short for 'Good on you!'.

one-eyed trouser snake
A penis.

one out of the box
also *one out of the bag*
A person or thing that is exceptional, usually
exceptionally good.

onkas *or* **onkaparingas**
The fingers. (Rhyming slang. Onkaparinga is a
brand of blanket.)

open-air wrestling
An insulting term for rugby. See **cross-country
wrestling**.

open slather
A situation or opportunity that is accessible to
anybody and everybody.

O.S.
Overseas.

Oscar Asche
Cash. (Rhyming slang. Oscar Asche was an
Australian stage actor, producer and writer.)

pack death
also *pack the shits*
To be very, very nervous or scared.

pack, gone to the
In a state of deterioration, failure or total
collapse.

Paddo
Short for Paddington, which is an inner suburb of Sydney.

pan
To criticise or condemn. Thus also *a panning*: 'The film got an absolute panning'.

pav
Short for pavlova, which is a popular meringue-based dessert created by an Australian chef in honour of the Russian ballerina Anna Pavlova.

pearler
A **purler**.

perhapser
An act with uncertain consequences. (Originally a cricketing term meaning a risky or hazardous stroke.)

perk
To vomit.

perve/perv
To watch or look at with lewd intent. *A perve* can be the action itself, or a person who does it habitually.

physio
Physiotherapy or a physiotherapist.

pigs! *or* **pig's arse!**
Rubbish! Nonsense!

pimp
As a noun, a person who informs or tell tales on
others. As a verb, to inform on or betray.

pinko
Politically speaking, a socialist or left-winger.
Depending on the context, it may also mean
drunk.

piss
1 Alcohol, especially beer. Thus *on the piss*
   means on a drinking spree.
2 The act of urinating.

piss-ant, drunk as a
Very drunk.

Confusingly, you can also be *as game as a piss-ant*, which means very courageous.

piss in someone's pocket
To fawn over or act sycophantically towards someone.

pisser
1 A pub.
2 A penis.
3 Something really bad – or something really good.

pisspot
A habitual drinker or drunkard.

plonk
Wine.

pocket rocket
A penis.

point Percy at the porcelain
To urinate.

point the bone at
To put a hex or jinx on.

poke
1 To punch or hit.
2 To have sexual intercourse.

pokies, the
Poker machines, which grace Australia's ever-increasing number of gambling venues.

pollie
A politician. See the comments at **barbie.**

pommie/pommy
also *pom*
Derogatory term for an English person. It is often used in insulting combinations, especially 'pommy bastard' and 'pommy poofter'.

poo/pooh, in the
In trouble.

pooey/poohy

Smelly, or disagreeable in some other way: 'in a pooey mood'.

poofter/pooftah

A male homosexual. It may, by extension, mean a weak, effeminate or artistic person. (Unusually, 'poofter' represents a lengthening of the cosmopolitan term 'poof': it is more common for Australians to abbreviate words.)

The term *poofter-bashing* describes homophobic behaviour or tendencies.

port

A suitcase or overnight bag. (Short for portmanteau.)

poultice
A lot of money: 'She earns a poultice in
that job'.

pozzie/possie
Position: 'Find yourself a comfortable pozzie'.

pull a swiftie/swifty
See **swiftie, pull a**.

pull someone's tit
To tease or make fun of someone.

pull up stakes
To leave or get ready to leave.

pull your head in!
An exhortation to be quiet or to mind one's own business.

purler
also *pearler*
Something outstandingly good or admirable: 'What a purler!'.

pushover
A person or thing which is very easy to do, master or acquire: 'That exam was a pushover'.

put the bite on
also *put the acid* or *the hard word on*
To put pressure on someone for something, especially money or sex.

put the mockers on
also *put the moz/mozz on*
To put a curse or jinx on.

quick quid, a
Money earned or acquired quickly; the Aussie
version of 'a fast buck'.

quince, get on one's
To vex or irritate.

quoit/coit
The backside or buttocks.

race off
To seduce.

rack off!
Go away!

Rafferty's rules
No rules at all, or no holds barred.

ragged
Tired or unwell: 'You look pretty ragged this morning'.

ratbag
An eccentric person, who may also be a little disreputable. *Ratbaggery* is the typical behaviour of such a person.

rat–shit
Awful: 'That hat looks rat-shit on you'.

razoo/rahzoo, not have a (brass)
To have no money or spare cash at all.

razzle
To steal.

red ned
Red wine, especially a cheap one.

Redfern, getting off at
Performing coitus interruptus. (On the Sydney
rail network, Redfern is one stop short of
Central Station.)

reef *or* **reef off**
To steal.

ridgy-didge
The truth, or the genuine article.

ring
The anus or backside.

ring-in
A substitute, especially a fraudulent one.

ripper
also *rip-snorter*
Something absolutely delightful or admirable:
'You little ripper!'.

roar someone up
also *roar shit out of*
To castigate someone severely.

Rock, the
Uluru, the monolith Ayers Rock which lies
south-west of Alice Springs in the Northern
Territory.

root
1 To have sexual intercourse.
2 To ruin or destroy.

rooted

1 Exhausted: 'I was up all night and now I'm absolutely rooted'.

2 Broken or ruined: 'This watch is rooted'.

rort

1 A ruse or scam. Thus *to rort* is to cheat or swindle.

2 A wild party.

rotten, get

To get drunk.

rough as bags
also *rough as guts*
Very rough or wild.

rough end of the pineapple, the
Unfair treatment or a difficult experience.
   For more of the same, see also **spin** or **trot, a rough**.

roughie
A rough or wild person or thing.

royal order, the
also *the order of the boot*
A sacking or rejection: 'The company was cutting back, so I got the royal order'.

R.S.
Short for **rat-shit.**

rubbish
To scoff at or put down.

rust-bucket
Something, especially a car, which is old
and in bad condition.

sambo
A sandwich.

sandgroper
A person from Western Australia.

sanger
A sausage.

sausage, to sink *or* **hide the**
also *sink* or *hide the sav* or *the weenie*
(of males) To have sexual intercourse.

scone
pronounced **skon**
The head.

scungy/skungy
Grubby or grotty.

semi
Short for just about any word with the prefix
semi-, but it is most likely to mean a semi-final
competition ('a footy semi'), a semi-trailer
('he drives a semi') or a semi-detached house
('a single-fronted semi').

send her down, Hughie
Please make it rain! ('Hughie' was traditionally a bush-dweller's epithet for God.)

septic tank
An American. (Rhyming slang for 'Yank'.)

serve, give someone a
To scold or berate. If you *cop a serve*, you are on the receiving end.

shaggin' wagon
also *sin bin*
A motor vehicle, often a van, fitted with drapes and other comforts and intended for sexual encounters.

shake hands with the wife's best friend
also *shake hands with the unemployed*
(of a man) To urinate.

shanghai
As a noun, a catapult. As a verb, to waylay or
steal.

shat off, be
To be fed up or really angry.

sheila
A girl or woman.

sheister/shyster
A swindler or dishonest person: 'Be careful, that guy's a real sheister!'.

sherbet
An alcoholic drink, but especially a beer: 'We're going to the pub for a few sherbets'.

she's *or* **she'll be apples!**
also *she's/she'll be jake* or *she's/she'll be right*
Don't worry, everything is (going to be) fine!

Like **no worries!**, this is a typical Aussie statement of breezy optimism. (Critics of the national character suggest it implies a reprehensible lack of commitment to the task at hand, let alone its outcome.)

shirt-lifter
A male homosexual.

shit
1 As a verb, to irritate or annoy. As a noun, a contemptible person.
2 When *shit hits the fan* you can expect trouble or unpleasantness to ensue.

shit a brick!
An exclamation of irritation or exasperation.

shit-can
To criticise or condemn.

shit-house
Very bad or awful: 'shit-house weather'.

shit-kicker
A person who does humble or degrading work.

shitty
1 Angry or hostile: 'He's really shitty with me'.
2 Bad, inferior or unwell: 'I admit I did a pretty shitty job'.

shoot through
To depart, especially hurriedly or without notice.

shouse
Short form of **shit-house**.

shout
To treat someone by paying for them: 'I'll shout you lunch'.

shutter-bug
A keen photographer.

sickie
Time off work, often through illness but sometimes through malingering.

silly as a two-bob watch
also *silly as a wheel* or *a hatful of worms*
Very silly indeed ('a two-bob watch' being a very cheap and probably not very reliable watch).

sink the slipper
To kick someone when they're down, literally or figuratively. (An Aussie variation on 'put the boot in'.)

skerrick, not a
Nothing or none at all: 'Sorry, there's not a skerrick of food in the house'.

skite
As a verb, to boast. As a noun, a conceited or boastful person.

skittle
To knock over.

slacker
A person who is lazy or shirks their obligations.

slag
1 To spit.
2 (sometimes *slag off*) To criticise or abuse.

sling off at
To insult or abuse: 'Slinging off at the umpire is great sport for footy spectators'.

slug
To charge: 'What did they slug you for the tickets?'.

smart–arse
A know-all.

snag short of a barbie
also *a sausage* or *a chop short of a barbie*
Not quite sane, or not very bright.

   Being *a few snags short* suggests that you
are seriously deficient in these areas.
Furthermore, you can be *a few sandwiches
short of a picnic* and *a few bricks short of
a load*.

snake–juice
Any very strong alcohol.

snake's hiss
Piss (both senses). (Rhyming slang.)

snaky/snakey
Irritable or bad-tempered.

soapie
A TV soap opera.

soda, a
Something which is very easy to do or achieve.

soft cop, a
also *a sweet cop*
A safe or easy time, task or occupation.

solid

Excessive or unfair: 'That's a bit solid!'.

sook

A coward or cry-baby. Thus *sooky* means wet or wimpish.

sool

To encourage to tackle or attack: 'They sooled their dog onto the intruder'.

southerly buster

A strong southerly wind.

spag

1 Spaghetti.

2 An Italian person or thing.

spear, get the

To be sacked. Hence to *give someone the spear*
is to sack them.

spear the bearded clam

(of a man) To have sex with a woman.

spider

A beverage composed of fizzy soft drink topped
with ice-cream.

spin *or* **trot, a**

1 An attempt or turn: 'Let's give it a spin'.
2 (as in *a fair spin*, *a rough spin*, etc.) A spell
  or period of (good or bad) luck, experiences
  or treatment: 'We've had a pretty rough
  spin lately'.

spit, the big
The act of vomiting.

spit the dummy
To totally lose patience and express one's anger,
indignation, etc.

spitting chips
Very angry.

sport
A term of address, along the same lines as
'mate' or 'cobber'.

spruiker
pronounced **sproo**-ker
A person who stands in front of a shop or stall
and eagerly promotes its wares to passers-by.

squib
1 A timid or cowardly person.
2 A fib.
3 Something that founders or fails.

squiz/squizz
A look: 'Let me have a squiz at it'.

stack on
To put on or perform: 'to stack on an act'.

steak and kidney
Sydney. (Rhyming slang.)

Steele Rudds
Potatoes. (Rhyming slang for 'spuds'. Steele
Rudd was the pseudonym of humorist Arthur
Hoey Davis, creator of the immortal Aussie rural
characters Dad and Dave.)

sticks, the
Far rural areas; the outback.

stickybeak
1 A busybody.
2 (also *sticky*) A look: 'Have a sticky at that haircut!'.

stinker
1 A very hot day.
2 Anything very difficult or unpleasant: 'That test was a stinker!'.

stir the possum
also *stir shit out of*
To intentionally upset things or cause trouble.

stirrer

A person who likes to **stir the possum**.

stone the crows!

A whimsical exclamation of amazement or disbelief. Variations include *starve the lizards!*, *stiffen the lizards!* and *speed the wombat!*

stonkered

1 Defeated, broken-down or exhausted: 'I was completely stonkered after the race'.
2 Drunk.

stoush

A fight, especially a fist-fight.

strike!

also *strike a light!*, *strike me dead!*, or
strike me pink!

An exclamation of amazement.

stubbie

Anything small or truncated, but especially
a small (375 ml) bottle of beer or (in the
form *stubbies*) a pair of very brief men's shorts.

stuff up

To botch or make a mess of things. *A stuff-up*
is what results when you do so.

stuffed

1 Exhausted: 'I feel totally stuffed today'.
2 Broken or useless: 'My computer is stuffed'.
3 Bothered: 'I can't be stuffed'.

sudden death on

Inclined to impose strict penalties or
punishment: 'That teacher is sudden death on
bubble-gum in the classroom'.

sunnies

Sunglasses.

super

1 Superannuation: 'Have you got much super
  stashed away?'.
2 Superphosphate.

swag
A lot of something, especially money: 'I hear you earn a swag in your new job'.

swiftie/swifty, pull a
also *do a swiftie*
To trick or deceive.

syphon the python
To **drain the dragon**.

take
A hoax or fraud: 'Lucky you didn't buy in: that scheme was just a take'.

take a piece out of
To lecture severely or scold: 'Dad really took a piece out of me!'.

tall poppy
A successful or celebrated person. This horticultural image reflects the Aussie tendency to cut such people down to size because of the perceived national preference for mediocrity.

Taz *or* **Tassie**
Tasmania.

tear into
To attack or tackle in a very determined way: 'They tore into their chores'.

technicolour yawn *or* **chunder**
also *multicolour yawn*
A vomiting.

things are crook at Tallarook
also *things are weak at Julia Creek*
Things are not good at all.

throw a map
also *throw sixers*
To vomit.

throw a seven
To collapse or die.

tickets on oneself
See **have tickets on oneself**.

tin-arse
also *tin-bum*
A very lucky or wealthy person.

tinnie/tinny
A can of beer. To *crack a tinnie* is to have a beer with a mate.

tizz up
To dress up or beautify.

tizzy
Flashy, gaudy or over-elaborate: 'a tizzy outfit'.

toey
Impatient or irritable.

togs
1 A swimming costume.
2 Clothes or *clobber*.

Toorak tractor
Disparaging term for a 4-wheel-drive, off-road vehicle owned by a city dweller and driven mainly in the suburbs.

Top End, the
The far north of the Northern Territory, around Darwin. *A Top-ender* is a person who lives there.

traps
See **around the traps**.

trimmer
An excellent or admirable person or thing: 'My new car's a little trimmer!'.

troppo, gone
Crazy, theoretically as the result of excessive tropical heat.

trot
as in *a fair trot*, *a rough trot*, etc.
See **spin**.

trots, the
1 Horse-trotting races: 'We're going to the trots tonight'.
2 Diarrhoea: 'I've got the trots'.

truckie
A long-distance truck driver.

true blue
Genuine, true or truthful.

true dinks
Really so or true: 'Is that true dinks?'. ('Dinks' is a diminutive of **dinkum**.)

tube
1 A can of beer.
2 Television.
3 To *send someone* or *something down the tube* means to sack or dismiss them.

tucker
Food.

turn
A party: 'There's a big turn on at the pub tonight'.

turps, on the
Drinking alcohol.

two bob
1 (in *not worth two bob*) Sub-standard, useless or worthless: 'A pollie's promise isn't worth two bob!'.
2 (in *two bob each way*) Hedging one's bets; a bet both ways.
3 See **silly as a two-bob watch**.
   ('Bob' is a colloquial term for a shilling or five decimal pence.)

two-dog night
A very cold night. (Originally implied that the night was so cold, one needed two dogs about oneself to keep warm.)

two-pot screamer
also *one-pot screamer*
A person who gets drunk on very little alcohol. (A 'pot' is a measurement of alcohol, usually beer, in some states.)

uey/uie, do a
See **yewie**.

unemployed, shake hands with the
See **shake hands with the wife's best friend**.

up a gum-tree
also *up a wattle*
1 Puzzled or bewildered.

2 Lost or off the track: 'No, you're really up a gum-tree there'.

up oneself
Conceited or arrogant: 'He's really up himself'.

up the ... (Bombers, Swans, Eagles, etc.)!
Come on! A spectator's shout of encouragement to his or her football team.

up the spout
also *up the chute* or *up the pole*
1 Useless or beyond repair: 'My computer's up the spout'.
2 Confused or confusing: 'Your argument is completely up the spout'.
3 (also *up the duff*) Pregnant.

up your jumper!
also *up you/yours for the rent!*
Aussie variants of the derisive or defiant retort
'Up you!'.

Vegemite-driller
A male homosexual.

Vinnies
St Vincent de Paul, a welfare organisation.

wacker/whacker
(usually friendly) A foolish or droll person.

wake-up, a
Wary, alert or on the ball, particularly as
regards potential trickery or deception:
'I'm a wake-up to you, mate!'.

walkabout, go
To wander off or disappear.

walloper
A policeman.

warwicks
Arms. (Rhyming slang: short for 'Warwick Farm[s]', a race-course in Sydney.)

wedgie
1 A wedge-tailed eagle.
2 A painful upwards pressure at the crotch, as when someone forcibly pulls up one's underpants or trousers..

weigh into
To attack or tackle energetically.

well under
Drunk: 'A bit pissed? I was well under!'.

westie
A person from the (historically poorer) western suburbs of Sydney or Melbourne.

wharfie
A wharf labourer.

wheelie
The larrikin-like act of violently accelerating one's car so that the wheels skid noisily. Also

used to describe the act of rearing up on the
back wheel of a bicycle.

whinge
To complain constantly and irritatingly.
A whinge is the act of doing this, and
a whinger is a person who does so too often.

white-ant
To encroach on someone else's territory.

white lady
1 Methylated spirits imbibed as an intoxicating
   drink.
2 Cocaine.

whizzer
Genitals or private parts.

whole box and dice
The lot; everything. (Aussie variant of
'the whole kit and kaboodle'.)

Windies, the
A cricket team from the West Indies.

wipe-off, to give the
To shun or dismiss: 'They gave us the wipe-off
once they got rich'.

wog

1 A germ or infection, especially the flu.
2 A disparaging term for a person from south-
eastern Europe or the Middle East.

won't have a bar of
Will not deal with or tolerate.

Woolloomooloo uppercut
A kick in the testicles.

woolly woofter
A homosexual. (Rhyming slang for 'poofter'.)

woop woop
Any very remote or alien place; the Aussie
equivalent of Timbuctoo.

work like Jacky
To work extremely hard. (Jacky was a traditional slang epithet for an Aboriginal.)

wowser
A killjoy or puritanical person, especially one who disapproves of drinking, gambling and other popular Aussie pastimes.

wrap/rap
also *wrap-up*
Praise or endorsement: 'The film got a big wrap'.

wrapped/rapt
Very ardent or enthusiastic: 'You got the tickets? I'm wrapped!'.

yakka/yacka
Work or effort: 'hard yakka'.

Yank tank
A large US-designed car, especially a showy
one.

Yankee shout
A round of drinks during which everyone pays for themselves: the Aussie equivalent of 'Dutch treat'.

yewie, do a
also *uey/uie*
To make a U-turn, literally or figuratively.

yike
A dispute or brawl.

yikes!
An exclamation of astonishment or alarm.

yippee beans
1 Baked beans.
2 Tablets containing a stimulant such as amphetamine.

youse
pronounced **yewz** or **yooce**
You: 'What are youse trying to say?'. Commonly used to imply the plural of 'you'.

zac/zack, not worth a
Totally worthless. (A *zac* was the name for a sixpenny coin in the days before decimal currency.)

ziff
A beard.